THE NEW BEST OF JAMES TAYLOR

CONTENTS

BARTENDER'S BLUES	54
DON'T LET ME BE LONELY TONIGHT	10
FIRE AND RAIN	60
GOLDEN MOMENTS	32
HER TOWN TOO	14
MEXICO	56
ONLY A DREAM IN RIO	40
SHOWER THE PEOPLE	6
SWEET BABY JAMES	2
UP ON THE ROOF	28
WALKING MAN	35
YOUR SMILING FACE	49
YOU'VE GOT A FRIEND	22

Front Cover Illustration: Brendan Walsh

© 1991 WARNER BROS. PUBLICATIONS INC.
All Rights Reserved

SHOWER THE PEOPLE

Words and Music by
JAMES TAYLOR

© 1975, 1976 COUNTRY ROAD MUSIC, INC.
All Rights Reserved

Vocal Ad Lib

They say in every life,
They say the rain must fall.
Just like a pouring rain,
Make it rain.
Love is sunshine.

HER TOWN TOO

Words and Music by
JAMES TAYLOR, JOHN DAVID SOUTHER
and WADDY WACHTEL

© 1981 COUNTRY ROAD MUSIC, INC., ICE AGE MUSIC, LEADSHEETLAND MUSIC
All Rights Reserved

18

GOLDEN MOMENTS

Words and Music by
JAMES TAYLOR

© 1976, 1980 COUNTRY ROAD MUSIC, INC.
All Rights Reserved

E9
Bm7
E9
burn - ing, so don't you let that yearn - ing pass you by.
ram - bl - ing on, stum - bl - ing a - round drunk down on the farm.
lis - ten to you, kiss - ing his ex - ist - ence good night.
A13
Dmaj7
A7sus4
Walk - ing man, walk - ing man
And the walk - ing man walks, he does - n't know
Walk - ing man, walk on
Dmaj7
A7sus4
Bm7
E9
A13
walks. Well, an - y oth - er man stops and talks,
noth - ing at all. Well, an - y oth - er man stops and talks,
by my door. Well, an - y oth - er man stops and talks,

To Coda
1.
Dmaj7
A7sus4
but the walk-ing man walks.
but the walk-ing man
Dmaj7
A7sus4
2.
Dmaj7
A7sus4
Well, the walks on by,
Dmaj7
Bm7
A
Gmaj7
F#m7
Em7
A7sus4
walk on by.
Most ev-er-y-bod-y's got seed to
Dmaj7
Gmaj7
F#7+5
sow.
It ain't al-ways eas-y for a weed to

Vocal Ad Lib

He's the walking man, born to walk,
Walk on, walking man.
Well now, would he have wings to fly,
Would he be free?
Golden wings against the sky.
Walking man, walk on by,
So long, walking man, so long.

ONLY A DREAM IN RIO

Words and Music by
JAMES TAYLOR

Moderately bright

More than a dis- tant land___ o- ver a shin- ing sea.___ More than a steam- ing breeze.___ More than a shin- ing eye.___

© 1985, 1986 COUNTRY ROAD MUSIC, INC. (BMI)
All Rights Reserved

Well, they tell___ me it's on-ly a dream__ in Ri-
more than a dream__ in Ri-

o. Noth-ing could be__ as sweet_ as it seems_ on this
o. I was there__ on the ver - y day__ and my

ver - y first__ day down.__ They re - mind me or
heart came back_ a - live.__ There was more,_____

have you so soon for - got - ten. Of - ten as not_ it's rot-
more than the sing - ing voic - es. More than the up__ turned fac-

ten inside and the mask soon slips a-way.
es. More

Strange taste of a trop-i-cal fruit. Ro-man-tic lan-guage of the

Por-tu-guese. Mel-o-dy on a wood-en flute.

Sum-mer boat-ing in the sum-mer breeze.

It's all right; you can stay a-sleep. You can close your eyes. You can trust the peo-ple, the par-a-dise. So call your keep-er and

Em7 Gmaj7 Asus4 D/F♯ G
3fr.
F♯m7 Amaj7 Bsus4 E/G♯ A
ten - der your good - byes. Oh, what a night, won-
Em7 A D/F♯ G Em7 A D/F♯
3fr.
F♯m7 B E/G♯ A F♯m7 B E/G♯
der - ful one in a mil - lion to - night. Fro - zen fire, Bra - zil -
G C(add D) D/F♯ G A
A D(add E) E/G♯ A B
ian stars. Oh, ho - ly South - ern Cross. Lat - er on
D/F♯ G Em7 A D/F♯ G
E/G♯ A F♯m7 B E/G♯ A
take you way down - town in a tin can. I can't

come down from the band-stand. I'm_ nev-er thrown_ for such a loss when they say:_ "Quan-do a nos-sa _ mãe acor-dar, an-da-reim-oz au sol. Quan-do a nos-sa _ mãe acor-dar can-tar-á pe-los ser-tão._ Quan-do a nos-sa_ *mae acor-dar, to-dos oz fili-os sa-be-rao, to-dos os fili-os sa-be-rão e re-go-zi-ja-rão."*

Caught in the rays of the ris- ing sun. On the run from the sol- dier's gun. Shout-ing out loud from the an-gry crowd, the mild,

D/F♯ G E/G♯ A D/F♯ G
D.S. 𝄋 al Coda ⊕
E/G♯ A F♯/A♯ B E/G♯ A
the wild and the hun - gry child. I'll tell you there's
Coda ⊕
C(add D) D/F♯ G A Bm7
D(add E) E/G♯ A B C♯m7
than the shin - ing eyes.
C(addD) D/F♯ G A G/B C(addD)
D(addE) E/G♯ A B A/C♯ D(addE)
But it's more
D/F♯ G A G/B C(addD)
E/G♯ A B A/C♯ D(addE)
than the shin - ing eyes.

More than the steam - ing breeze.
More than the con - crete Christ.
o - ver a shin - ing sea.
More like an - oth - er time.

More than the hid - den hills.
More than a dis - tant land.
More than a hun - gry child.
More than a mil - lion years.

More than a mil - lion years.

Repeat and fade

YOUR SMILING FACE

Words and Music by
JAMES TAYLOR

Moderately, with a beat

Whenever I see your smiling face, I have to smile myself, because I love you; yes, I do.

© 1977 COUNTRY ROAD MUSIC, INC.
All Rights Reserved

And when you give me that pretty little pout, it turns me inside out. There's something about you, baby; I don't know. Isn't it amazing a man like me can feel this way?

*Move capo to 4th fret.

you. And I thank my luck-y stars that you are who you are and not just an-oth-er love-ly la-dy sent down to break my heart. Is-n't it a-maz-ing a man like me can feel this way? Tell me how much long-er; it can grow

sheet music

BARTENDER'S BLUES

Words and Music by
JAMES TAYLOR

folks with their backs to the wall.
pack up and mail in my key.
stranded at the edge of the sea.

But I need four walls a-round me to hold my life; to keep me from going astray; and a honky-tonk angel to hold me tight to keep me from slipping away.

I can
Now, the slipping away.

MEXICO

Words and Music by
JAMES TAYLOR

Moderately

© 1975 COUNTRY ROAD MUSIC, INC.
All Rights Reserved

y's still running your state-side games. Lose your load,
back home shaking like a live wire.
back home don't want to talk on the phone. She gets

leave your mind behind, Baby James.
Sleep-y señorita with the eyes on fire.
a long letter, sends back a post-card; times are hard.

Whoa, Mex-i-co, it sounds so sim-ple I've just
Whoa, Mex-i-co, you sound so sweet with the sun
Whoa, down in Mex-i-co, I've nev-er real-ly been, so I don't

got to go. Sun's so hot, I forgot
sinking low. Moon's so bright, like to light
really know. Whoa,

to go home.
up the night.
Mexico, I

1. Guess I'll have to go now.

2. Make ev'ry-thing all right.

3. guess I'll have to say: Whoa, Mex-i-co, I've never really been, but I'd sure like to go. Whoa, Mex-i-co, I guess I'll have to go now.

Repeat and fade

Whoa, Mex-i-co.

Fire and Rain

Words and Music by
JAMES TAYLOR

Moderately

Just yes-ter-day morn-ing, they let me know you were gone.
look down up-on me, Je-sus. You got-ta help me make a stand.

Su-zanne, the plans they made put an end to you.
You just got to see me through an-oth-er day.

Copyright © 1969, 1970, 1978 EMI Blackwood Music Inc. and Country Road Music, Inc.
All rights controlled and administered by EMI Blackwood Music Inc.
International Copyright Secured   Made in U.S.A.
All Rights Reserved

A Em7 D A
C Gm7 F C
5 fr.
I walked out this morn-ing and I wrote down this song.
My bod - y's ach-ing and my time is at hand.
E Gmaj7(no 3rd)
G B♭maj7(no 3rd)
I just can't re - mem-ber who to send — it to.
And I won't make it an - y oth - er way.
D D/C♯ Bm7 D/E A
F F/E Dm7 F/G C
I've seen fire and I've — seen rain. I've seen
mf
D D/C♯ Bm7 D/E A
F F/E Dm7 F/G C
sun-ny days — that I thought — would nev - er end. —

I've seen lonely times when I could not find a friend.
But I always thought that I'd see you again.
Won't you
Been walking my mind to an easy time, my back turned towards the sun.

63

Lord knows, when the cold wind blows, it-'ll turn your head a-round.

Well, there's hours of time on the tel-e-phone line to talk a-bout things to come: sweet dreams and fly-ing ma-chines in piec-es on the ground.

D.S. al Coda

see you, ba - by, one more time a - gain, now.

Thought I'd see you one more time a - gain.

There's just a few things com - ing my way this time a - round.

Repeat and fade